Contents

Introduction to Architectural Entrepreneurship

In today's increasingly competitive and dynamic world, the field of architecture has undergone a remarkable transformation. No longer limited to designing buildings, it has evolved into a multifaceted industry that demands a strong entrepreneurial mindset to thrive. Architectural entrepreneurship combines the creative and innovative aspects of architectural design with the strategic thinking and business acumen of an entrepreneur. In this chapter, we will delve even deeper into the concept of architectural entrepreneurship, providing a comprehensive understanding of the opportunities and challenges it entails.

Traditionally, architecture was seen as a profession centered around providing design and construction solutions to clients. However, over the years, architects have realized the need to expand their role beyond the realm of technical expertise.

They now see themselves as more than just

designers; they also embrace the identity of entrepreneurs. This shift in mindset is driven by a desire to create a sustainable and profitable architectural practice that goes beyond delivering projects, and seeks to make a positive impact on the built environment and society as a whole.

At its core, architectural entrepreneurship is about going beyond the traditional boundaries of architecture and capitalizing on business opportunities. Architects must not only be adept at designing buildings but also possess the vision and acumen to create a thriving and financially viable firm. This involves identifying market trends, anticipating client needs, and developing innovative solutions that differentiate their practice from competitors.

To be successful architectural entrepreneurs, professionals must possess a keen eye for recognizing market gaps and unmet client demands. They must leverage their creative skills and design expertise to create unique and compelling solutions that resonate with clients.

By identifying and capitalizing on these

opportunities, architectural entrepreneurs can drive the growth and success of their practice.

Achieving success in architectural entrepreneurship also requires a willingness to take calculated risks. Building a thriving architectural practice demands architects to step outside their comfort zones and embrace uncertainty. They must dare to challenge conventional thinking, explore new ideas, and push the boundaries of design. By taking risks, architectural entrepreneurs can foster innovation and create breakthrough solutions that set their firms apart.

Moreover, architectural entrepreneurship is rooted in the ability to build and nurture relationships. Architects must develop strong connections with clients, industry partners, and other professionals. Networking and collaboration are vital in the field of architecture, as they foster creativity and pave the way for new opportunities. Successful architectural entrepreneurs understand the value of

relationships and invest time and effort in

cultivating a robust network of contacts.

In this extended version of the book, we will delve even further into various aspects of architectural entrepreneurship, providing actionable insights and practical advice to aspiring architectural entrepreneurs. We will explore topics such as business planning, legal and financial considerations, marketing strategies, project management, fostering innovation, collaboration, and scaling up your practice for growth and expansion.

To build a successful architectural practice, entrepreneurs must develop a visionary mindset that allows them to see beyond the immediate project and envision the future. They must synthesize their design skills with strategic thinking to create a compelling vision for their practice, aligning it with the evolving needs of the market and society. By articulating this vision, architectural entrepreneurs can attract clients, talent, and strategic partners who share their values and aspirations.

Additionally, a solid foundation is essential for any

entrepreneurial venture. Architectural entrepreneurs must establish a sound business plan that outlines their goals, target market, competitive advantage, and financial projections. This plan should serve as a roadmap that guides their decisions, ensures operational efficiency, and drives the long-term success of the practice.

Legal and financial considerations are also critical in architectural entrepreneurship. Architects must navigate legal regulations, licensing requirements, insurance, contracts, and intellectual property rights. They must have an understanding of financial management, budgeting, cash flow, and project costing to ensure their practice remains financially stable and profitable. Collaborating with legal and financial professionals can provide valuable guidance in these areas.

Marketing strategies play a pivotal role in the success of an architectural practice. Architectural entrepreneurs must develop a compelling brand identity that reflects their unique approach and values. They must leverage both traditional and digital marketing channels to reach potential clients and establish their presence in the industry. Effective marketing not only generates leads but also helps build a reputation and credibility that attracts clients and fosters sustainable growth.

Project management skills are vital in architectural entrepreneurship. Architects must ensure that projects are completed within the agreed-upon timeframe and budget while maintaining the highest quality standards. Effective project management involves managing resources, coordinating with various stakeholders, and employing efficient processes and technologies. By delivering projects successfully, architectural entrepreneurs establish a track record that enhances their reputation and helps secure future contracts.

Fostering a culture of innovation is critical to architectural entrepreneurship. Architects must embrace emerging technologies, sustainability practices, and interdisciplinary collaborations to drive creativity and deliver cutting-edge solutions. They must continuously update their knowledge and skills, encouraging their team members to do the same. Embracing a culture of lifelong learning and innovation not only keeps architectural entrepreneurs ahead of the curve but also enables them to better serve their clients and adapt to changing market dynamics.

As architectural practices grow and succeed, architectural entrepreneurs must navigate the challenges of scaling up their business. This may involve expanding their team, diversifying service offerings, or entering new markets. Strategic planning and effective leadership become even more crucial at this stage to ensure sustainable growth while maintaining the highest standards of design and client satisfaction.

Architectural entrepreneurship is an exciting and challenging journey that demands a unique blend of creativity, business acumen, and a passion for design. This book aims to equip aspiring architectural entrepreneurs with the knowledge, tools, and strategies needed to build successful and sustainable architectural practices. By exploring the intricacies of the architectural industry and the intersecting realms of design and business, readers will gain a deeper understanding of how to make informed decisions that drive the growth and success of their practice.

Embarking on the path of architectural entrepreneurship requires enthusiasm, curiosity, and a willingness to embrace change. It is a journey that presents immense opportunities for personal and professional growth, as well as the chance to make a lasting impact on the built environment. As we traverse through the chapters, we invite you to immerse yourself in the world of architectural entrepreneurship, uncovering the potential within you to become a thriving architectural entrepreneur. Together, we will pave the way for innovative solutions and a brighter future for the field of architecture.

The Entrepreneurial Mindset in Architecture

The entrepreneurial mindset is a transformative approach that goes beyond simply being a talented architect. It requires a holistic understanding of business principles and a proactive attitude that embraces opportunities for growth and innovation. Architects with an entrepreneurial mindset are better equipped to navigate the challenges of the industry, seize new prospects, and create a lasting impact on the built environment.

One of the key elements of the entrepreneurial mindset is the ability to identify and capitalize on emerging trends. Staying ahead of the curve requires architects to continuously research and analyze the market, keeping a close eye on social, economic, and technological shifts. By doing so, they can identify emerging demands, such as sustainable design, smart buildings, or

wellness-focused spaces, and position themselves as experts in these areas. This not only allows architects to attract a niche audience but also ensures they remain relevant and influential in the field.

In addition to identifying trends, entrepreneurial architects actively contribute to shaping them. They are not content with following the mainstream design principles but seek to challenge and redefine the status quo. These architects are driven by a passion for innovation and experimentation, pushing the boundaries of design to create groundbreaking structures that inspire and captivate. They explore new materials, construction techniques, and technologies to create extraordinary spaces that not only meet functional requirements but also address societal, environmental, and cultural needs. By constantly seeking novel solutions, entrepreneurial architects become thought leaders, inspiring others in the industry and driving forward the collective evolution of architectural design.

While being trendsetters, architects with an entrepreneurial mindset also maintain a strong focus on meeting their clients' needs and aspirations. They recognize that architecture is ultimately about people and how they interact with their surroundings. With a deep understanding of their clients' goals, values, and lifestyles, these architects actively engage with clients throughout the design process. They foster a collaborative environment, encouraging open communication and dialogue to ensure that the final design aligns with the clients' vision and exceeds their expectations. By placing the client at the heart of every project, entrepreneurial architects deliver personalized and meaningful architectural experiences, creating a lasting impact on the lives of those who inhabit the spaces they design.

Moreover, entrepreneurial architects embrace a comprehensive approach to their work. They understand that architecture is not limited to the design phase but encompasses the entire life cycle of a project. By expanding their

services beyond design and venturing into development, construction management, or real estate investment, these architects have greater control over the process and outcome of their projects. Engaging in these additional roles allows them to manifest their vision holistically, from the initial concept to the final construction. This comprehensive approach not only enhances their impact but also provides additional revenue streams and business opportunities, ensuring their long-term success.

Collaboration is another essential aspect of the entrepreneurial mindset. These architects recognize the power of interdisciplinary collaboration and actively seek partnerships with engineers, contractors, and consultants. By bringing together diverse expertise and perspectives, they co-create outstanding projects that seamlessly integrate all elements of the built environment. Collaborative relationships foster innovation and enable entrepreneurial architects to tackle complex challenges, leverage the latest technologies,

and deliver exceptional results. By embracing collaboration and building strong networks,

architects with an entrepreneurial mindset position themselves as leaders in the industry, cultivating a reputation for excellence and pushing the boundaries of what architecture can achieve.

Lastly, the entrepreneurial mindset requires architects to be resilient, adaptable, and agile. The industry is constantly evolving, influenced by economic fluctuations, technological advancements, and societal shifts. Architects with this mindset embrace change and are quick to adapt their strategies and services to align with evolving demands. They anticipate future trends and proactively seek new opportunities for growth and innovation. These architects are not deterred by setbacks but instead view them as learning experiences and stepping stones towards success. Their adaptability allows them to thrive in a dynamic industry, seize emerging opportunities, and create a lasting impact on the built environment.

In conclusion, the entrepreneurial mindset is a game-changer for architects who wish to excel in their careers and make a lasting impact. By proactively identifying trends, setting new standards, embracing client-centered approaches, expanding services, fostering collaboration, and being resilient, adaptable, and agile, architects with an entrepreneurial mindset not only create aesthetically pleasing and functional spaces but also shape the future of the architectural field. Moreover, by embracing this mindset, architects unlock their full potential to innovate, diversify, and achieve remarkable success both professionally and personally.

Creating a Vision and Mission for Your Architectural Firm

Your vision and mission serve as the guiding principles for your architectural firm. They define its purpose, values, and goals, and provide a clear direction for the future. In this extended chapter, we will explore how to create a compelling vision and mission for your architectural firm that will inspire your team, attract clients, and set you apart from the competition.

1. Defining Your Vision:

A vision is a statement that describes the long-term aspirations of your architectural firm. It should capture the essence of what you strive to achieve and where you envision the firm heading in the next several years. Here are some key considerations to help define your vision:

a. Consider the future impact of your architectural designs: Think about the legacy you want to leave behind through your creations.

How do you aspire to impact the built environment?

Do you want to design sustainable buildings that reduce environmental impact? Or perhaps you aim to create spaces that foster human connection and well-being? Your vision should reflect the specific issues or challenges you want to address with your architectural designs.

b. Reflect on your values and principles: Consider the core values and principles that underpin your firm's work. What are your fundamental beliefs and philosophies that guide decision-making and shape your firm's culture? These values may include creativity, innovation, sustainability, community engagement, or client satisfaction. Your vision should align with these values and demonstrate how they will be manifest in your firm's future achievements.

c. Envision the growth and evolution of your firm: Look beyond immediate, short-term goals and imagine how you want your architectural firm to evolve over time. Visualize the size, scope, and

reputation you want it to achieve. Consider the types of projects, clients, and industries you aspire to work with.

This will help you define the trajectory of your firm and establish the benchmarks you aim to reach.

2. Crafting Your Mission:

While the vision sets the long-term direction, the mission statement focuses on the day-to-day operations and purpose of your architectural firm. It should articulate who you serve, what you do, and why you do it. Here's how to craft an impactful mission statement:

a. Identify your target clients and services: Pinpoint the specific needs and desires of your target clients. Who are your ideal clients, and what are their aspirations? Understanding their pain points and aspirations will help you determine the services and solutions your firm can provide to meet their needs. This customer-centric approach ensures that your

mission statement caters to your clients' aspirations.

b. Define your unique approach: What sets your firm apart from other architectural practices?

Consider your firm's unique approach, perspective, or skills that give you a competitive edge. It could be your expertise in a particular architectural style, your focus on sustainable design, or your specialization in adaptive reuse projects. Highlighting this differentiation in your mission statement showcases your expertise and offers a clear value proposition to potential clients.

c. Express your desired impact: Articulate the impact you aim to have through your architectural designs. How do you want your work to positively affect the lives of those who experience your spaces? Do you strive to create inspiring environments that enhance productivity and well-being? Or perhaps you aim to design public spaces that foster inclusivity and social connection? Clearly conveying the intended

impact of your work in your mission statement shows your commitment to making a difference.

d. Align with the architectural community: Consider how you want your firm to contribute to the wider architectural community. This might involve sharing knowledge and expertise through

publications, participating in industry events, or mentoring aspiring architects. Aligning your firm's mission with the larger architectural community demonstrates your dedication to the profession and your ongoing commitment to enhancing the practice and understanding of architecture.

In crafting your mission statement, remember to keep it concise, customer-focused, and memorable. It should capture the essence of your firm's identity and resonate with both clients and employees.

3. Aligning Vision and Mission:

To ensure the cohesiveness of your vision and mission statements, they should be

interconnected and mutually supportive. Here are

some points to consider in aligning your vision and mission:

a. Continuously evaluate and evolve: Regularly review and refine your vision and mission statements as your architectural firm evolves. As you grow and adapt to changing market dynamics, your vision and mission should remain

relevant and reflect your firm's current goals and values. Periodically revisit and refine these statements to ensure that they accurately represent your firm's objectives.

b. Set measurable goals and objectives: Establish measurable goals and objectives that align with your vision and mission. These goals will serve as progress markers on your firm's journey towards realizing its long-term aspirations. Make sure these goals are specific, realistic, and time-bound. Regularly track and analyze your progress to stay on the right path.

c. Involve your team in the process: Engage your employees in the development and implementation of your vision and mission. Encourage their input and involvement to foster a sense of ownership and commitment. Conduct brainstorming sessions or workshops where team members can contribute their ideas and perspectives. This inclusive approach cultivates a collaborative and supportive work environment.

d. Embrace flexibility and adaptability: Foster a culture that embraces your vision and mission.

Encourage continuous learning, innovation, and adaptability, allowing your firm to evolve while maintaining its core values. Empower your team to think creatively and seek innovative solutions that align with your firm's purpose. Develop an internal communication strategy to ensure that your vision and mission are effectively communicated and understood by every team member.

4. Communicating and Implementing Your Vision and Mission:

Once you have defined your vision and mission, it is crucial to effectively communicate and implement them throughout your firm. Here are some key strategies to consider:

a. Communicate externally: Share your vision and mission statements on your website, in marketing materials, and during client meetings. Make sure they are visible and easily accessible to potential clients who want to understand your firm's values and aspirations. Clearly articulate your unique selling points and how your architectural designs can address the needs of your target clients.

b. Communicate internally: Ensure that your vision and mission statements are communicated and understood by your internal team members. Regularly remind them of the firm's purpose and goals during team meetings, workshops, or through internal newsletters. Consider creating visual representations of your vision and mission statements that can be displayed in your office

spaces as a constant reminder for your team.

c. Embed it in your operations and decision-making: Incorporate your vision and mission into your firm's day-to-day operations by aligning these statements with your decision-making processes. Make sure that project selection, team assignments, and resource allocation are in line with your firm's objectives. Regularly evaluate projects, processes, and initiatives to ensure they are in alignment with your vision and mission, making any necessary adjustments to stay on track.

d. Celebrate successes and milestones: Recognize and celebrate achievements that demonstrate progress towards your firm's vision and mission. Share success stories within your firm, highlight

projects that effectively embody your values, and show how your architectural designs have positively impacted clients and communities.

Celebrating these milestones reinforces your vision and mission and motivates your team to continue working towards their realization.

By carefully crafting and aligning your vision and mission statements, you can establish a strong foundation for your architectural firm's success. Stay true to your core values and beliefs, and let your vision and mission guide your firm's decisions and actions. Regularly revisit and refine these statements to ensure they remain relevant and inspiring.

In addition to defining your vision and mission, it is important to communicate and implement them effectively. Here are some strategies to consider:

1. Engage your team: Involve your employees in the process of developing and implementing your vision and mission. Encourage their input and ideas, and make sure they feel a sense of ownership and commitment.

This can be done through team meetings, workshops, or even individual conversations. By involving your team, you can tap into their expertise and perspective, leading to a more comprehensive and effective vision and mission.

2. Create a shared purpose: Clearly communicate your vision and mission to your team and emphasize how their individual roles contribute to

the overall goals of the firm. Help them understand how their work aligns with the vision and mission, and how it contributes to the success of the firm. This shared purpose will foster a sense of motivation and engagement among your team members.

3. Provide resources and support: Ensure that your team has the necessary resources and support to fulfill the objectives of your vision and mission. This may include providing training, tools, or mentoring to help them succeed. By investing in your team's growth and providing the necessary support, you are setting them up for success and reinforcing the importance of your vision and mission.

4. Communicate externally: Share your vision and mission with your clients, partners, and the wider community. Use your website, social media platforms, and other marketing materials to

clearly communicate what your firm stands for and the impact it aims to make. Consistently reinforce your brand messaging and values in all external communications to attract clients who align with your vision and mission.

5. Foster collaboration and innovation: Create a culture of collaboration and innovation within your firm. Encourage your team members to share ideas, experiment with new approaches,

and learn from each other's experiences. By fostering a collaborative and innovative environment, you are more likely to achieve your vision and mission through fresh thinking and continuous improvement.

6. Measure progress and celebrate milestones: Establish key performance indicators (KPIs) that align with your vision and mission, and regularly measure and track your progress. Celebrate achievements and milestones, both small and large, to keep your team motivated and engaged.

By acknowledging and celebrating successes, you are reinforcing the importance of your vision

and mission and inspiring your team to continue working towards its realization.

Remember, your vision and mission are not simply statements on paper—they should act as a compass for your firm's actions, decisions, and behaviors. By aligning your team around them and consistently reinforcing them, you can create a strong sense of purpose and direction that will guide your architectural firm towards success.

Building a Strong Foundation: Business Planning and Startup Essentials

Starting your own architectural firm is an exciting venture that requires careful planning and strategic decision-making. Establishing a strong foundation through effective business planning and startup essentials is crucial for the long-term success and sustainability of your firm. In this chapter, we will delve into the essential elements of business planning and provide an in-depth exploration of the startup essentials necessary for setting up and running an architectural firm effectively.

1. Defining Your Business Model

To start your architectural firm, it is imperative to define your business model clearly. Take the time to determine the specific architectural services you want to offer, whether it's residential, commercial, institutional, or specialized areas like sustainable design or historic preservation.

Understanding your niche
will allow you to target your marketing efforts
and effectively position your firm in the industry.

Additionally, consider conducting thorough
research to identify your target market, which is
crucial for developing effective marketing
strategies. Look into factors such as
demographics, geographic location, and market
trends to identify potential clients who align with
your firm's expertise and vision. This knowledge
will shape your marketing strategies and help
you tailor your services to meet the needs of
your target audience.

2. Crafting a Comprehensive Business Plan

Creating a well-crafted and comprehensive
business plan is essential for guiding the growth
and development of your architectural firm. A
robust business plan highlights your firm's
mission, vision, and goals, providing a roadmap
for success. Consider including the following key
components in your business plan:

a. Executive Summary: This concise overview introduces your firm's mission, vision, and primary goals. It should captivate readers and provide a snapshot of your firm's value proposition.

b. Company Description: Delve into the details of your firm's background and history. Provide information about the services you offer, highlighting your firm's unique value proposition and the qualities that set you apart from your competitors.

c. Market Analysis: Conduct an in-depth analysis of the architectural industry, including current trends, challenges, and growth opportunities. Understand your target market and potential clients, and identify their needs and preferences.

d. Competitive Analysis: Evaluate your competitors' strengths, weaknesses, and market position to understand the landscape in which you want to operate. Identify ways to differentiate yourself and develop a competitive advantage.

e. Marketing and Sales Strategies: Develop a robust marketing plan to reach and attract potential clients. Outline your strategies for marketing your services, acquiring clients, and building strong industry relationships. Consider incorporating digital marketing techniques, networking events, and referrals in your approach.

f. Organization and Management: Specify your firm's structure and key team members. Clarify the roles and responsibilities of each team member, emphasizing their qualifications and expertise. This section should demonstrate your firm's organizational capacity and the strengths of your team.

g. Financial Projections: Project your firm's financial performance over the next few years, including revenue, expenses, cash flow, and profitability. Create realistic forecasts based on thorough market research and sound financial analysis.

h. Implementation Plan: Outline the specific steps you will take to execute your strategies and achieve your business goals. Detail your timeline, budget, and the resources required to reach each milestone.

Consider seeking guidance from a business consultant or mentor with expertise in the architectural industry to refine your business plan and ensure it aligns with industry best practices.

3. Securing Adequate Financing

Before launching your architectural firm, it is vital to secure the necessary financing to cover your startup and operational costs. Evaluate the various expenses involved, including office space, equipment, software licenses, salaries, marketing, and professional insurance. Prepare a detailed budget that takes into account both short-term and long-term financial needs.

Exploring various financing options can help you secure the necessary funds:

a. Self-Funding: Consider utilizing personal savings or investments to start your firm. This option gives you full control over your finances but may limit your initial resources.

b. Bank Loans: Approach banks or credit unions to secure a business loan. To increase your chances of approval, prepare a comprehensive loan proposal that outlines your firm's financial viability and growth potential.

c. Small Business Administration (SBA) Loans: The SBA offers loans specifically designed for small businesses. These loans often have advantageous terms and lower interest rates. Research the SBA loan programs and requirements to determine if they align with your firm's needs.

d. Grants and Scholarships: Research and apply for grants and scholarships geared towards small architectural firms and sustainable design initiatives. These options can provide additional financial support and recognition for your firm.

4. Setting Up a Functional and Inspiring Office Space

Creating a functional and inspiring work environment sets the stage for productivity and creativity within your architectural firm. When selecting an office space, consider the following factors:

a. Location: Choose a location that is convenient for both your employees and clients. Ideally, it should be easily accessible by public transportation, have ample parking facilities, and be situated in an area known for its architectural and design community.

b. Space Design and Layout: When designing your office layout, prioritize functionality, collaboration, and creativity. Allocate adequate space for architectural design workstations, project collaboration areas, meeting rooms, and storage. Keep in mind the importance of natural light and open spaces in fostering creativity.

c. Ergonomics and Comfort: Invest in ergonomic furniture and equipment to promote health and well-being among your team members. Create comfortable areas for relaxation and break times to foster a positive work environment.

d. Technology Infrastructure: Establish a robust technology infrastructure that supports seamless communication, collaboration, and project management within your firm. Invest in reliable hardware, high-speed internet, and robust cybersecurity measures to protect your firm's data.

e. Sustainable Practices: Consider incorporating sustainable design principles into your office space. Utilize energy-efficient lighting, implement recycling programs, and choose environmentally friendly materials whenever possible. Showcasing your firm's commitment to sustainability can attract like-minded clients and bolster your reputation.

5. Building an Outstanding Team

As your architectural firm grows, assembling a team of talented and dedicated professionals becomes crucial for delivering exceptional design and service. Follow these strategies for building an outstanding team:

a. Clearly Define Job Descriptions and Roles: Clearly define the expectations, responsibilities, and qualifications for each role within your firm. This will attract candidates who are the right fit for your team and minimize misunderstandings.

b. Conduct Thorough Interviews and Assessments: Develop a comprehensive interview process to assess candidates' technical skills and cultural fit. Utilize practical exercises or design tests to evaluate candidates' capabilities and compatibility with the firm's values.

c. Foster a Collaborative and Supportive Work Culture: Create a positive work environment that fosters collaboration, communication, and continuous growth. Encourage open and transparent communication among team members, and provide ongoing opportunities for professional development and advancement.

d. Offer Competitive Compensation and Benefits: To attract and retain talented professionals, ensure that your firm offers competitive salaries and benefits. Stay informed about market rates to ensure you provide fair compensation for your team members' skills and experiences.

e. Encourage Continuing Education: Support and encourage your team members to engage in ongoing professional development. Provide opportunities for attending conferences, workshops, and industry events to stay up-to-date with the latest architectural trends and innovations.

6. Establishing Legal and Administrative Procedures

Establishing legal and administrative procedures is essential to ensure compliance and protect your firm's interests. Engage with legal and financial professionals experienced in the architectural industry to guide you through the process. Here are some key considerations:

a. Registering your Firm: Determine the legal structure of your firm (e.g., sole proprietorship, partnership, or corporation) and register it with the appropriate government agencies. Obtain all necessary licenses and permits to operate legally in your jurisdiction.

b. Contracts and Agreements: Develop standard contract templates for your architectural services. These contracts should outline the scope of work, payment terms, intellectual property rights, and any other important details. Consult with an attorney to ensure your contracts are comprehensive and legally binding.

c. Insurance: Obtain professional liability insurance to protect your firm against claims of negligence or errors and omissions. Consider other types of insurance, such as general liability insurance and property insurance, to safeguard your firm's assets and mitigate potential risks.

d. Intellectual Property Protection: Understand the intellectual property rights associated with your architectural designs. Register your firm's trademarks and copyrights to protect your brand identity and original work.

e. Financial and Accounting Processes: Implement robust financial and accounting processes to ensure accurate record-keeping and compliance. Consider hiring a professional accountant or bookkeeper to manage your firm's financials, including invoicing, payroll, taxes, and financial reporting.

f. Data Management and Security: Establish secure data management practices to protect your firm's sensitive information and client data. Implement data backup systems, firewalls, and encryption technologies to minimize the risk of data breaches or cyber attacks.

g. Human Resources and Employee Policies: Develop comprehensive employee policies and procedures to govern your firm's operations. This includes policies related to employee benefits, performance evaluations, vacation and time off, and disciplinary processes. Adhere to all labor laws governing employment practices and maintain a safe and inclusive work environment.

7. Implementing Effective Project Management Systems

Efficient project management is crucial for delivering architectural projects on time and within budget. Implementing effective project management systems helps streamline workflows, improve communication, and ensure client satisfaction. Consider the following tips for successful project management:

a. Project Planning and Scheduling: Create detailed project plans, outlining tasks, deliverables, milestones, and deadlines. Utilize project management tools, such as Gantt charts or Kanban boards, to visualize project timelines and allocate resources effectively.

b. Communication and Collaboration: Establish clear channels of communication with clients, consultants, and team members. Utilize collaboration tools and software to facilitate file sharing, feedback, and real-time updates. Regularly communicate project progress and address any concerns or issues promptly.

c. Budget and Cost Management: Develop a robust budgeting process to track project costs and expenses. Regularly monitor project finances to ensure projects remain within budget. Implement protocols for requesting change orders or revisions to minimize scope creep and maintain profitability.

d. Quality Control and Quality Assurance: Implement comprehensive quality control measures to ensure the highest standards of design and construction. Conduct regular inspections and evaluations to identify and address any potential quality issues.

Implement quality assurance processes to continuously improve project outcomes.

e. Documentation and Record-Keeping: Establish a system for effective documentation and record-keeping. Maintain detailed project files, including drawings, specifications, correspondence, and client approvals. This ensures easy access to project-related information and protects your firm in case of disputes or claims.

8. Marketing and Promoting Your Firm

Effective marketing is essential for attracting new clients and establishing your firm's reputation in the architectural industry. Here are some strategies for successfully marketing and promoting your architectural firm:

a. Develop a Strong Brand Identity: Create a visually compelling and cohesive brand identity that reflects your firm's values, vision, and expertise. Design a professional logo, website, and marketing materials that convey your firm's unique personality and style.

b. Digital Marketing: Leverage digital marketing channels to increase your firm's online visibility. Develop a user-friendly website that showcases your portfolio, projects, and client testimonials. Implement search engine optimization (SEO) techniques to improve your website's rankings in search results. Utilize social media platforms, email marketing campaigns, and content marketing to engage with potential clients and share valuable industry insights.

c. Networking and Industry Engagement: Attend industry events, conferences, and trade shows to connect with potential clients and industry professionals. Join professional organizations and actively participate in industry discussions and forums to establish your firm as a thought leader.

d. Referrals and Client Testimonials: Encourage satisfied clients to refer your firm to their network. Develop a referral program that incentivizes clients to recommend your services.

Request and showcase client testimonials and reviews on your website and social media platforms to build trust and credibility.

e. Thought Leadership and Content Creation: Position yourself and your firm as industry experts by sharing valuable insights and knowledge through thought leadership content. Write articles, blog posts, or whitepapers that address relevant architectural topics or trends. Consider guest speaking or hosting webinars to share your expertise with a wider audience.

In conclusion, building a strong foundation for your architectural firm involves strategic business planning and implementing essential startup practices. Define your business model, craft a comprehensive business plan, secure adequate financing, set up a functional office space, build an outstanding team, establish legal and administrative procedures, implement effective project management systems, and market your firm effectively.

By following these best practices, you can position your firm for long-term success and growth in the architectural industry.

Navigating the Legal and Financial Aspects of an Architectural Firm

Running a successful architectural firm requires not only creative design skills but also a solid understanding of the legal and financial aspects of the industry. In this chapter, we will explore key considerations and best practices for navigating the legal and financial landscape of your architectural firm. From understanding contracts and liability to managing finances and taxes, this chapter will provide valuable insights to help you establish and maintain a financially stable and legally compliant architectural practice.

1. Legal Considerations:
a. Choosing the Right Legal Structure:
The legal structure you choose for your architectural firm will have long-lasting

implications for liability, taxes, and operational flexibility. Let's take a closer look at some common options:

- Sole Proprietorship: A sole proprietorship is the simplest structure where you are the sole owner. However, bear in mind that your personal assets might be at risk in case of any liabilities.
- Partnership: Like a sole proprietorship, partnerships involve shared ownership, but it is important to define responsibilities, profit-sharing, and exit strategies through a well-drafted partnership agreement.
- Limited Liability Company (LLC): An LLC provides both limited liability and operational flexibility. Members are typically not personally liable for the debts and liabilities of the company.
- Professional Corporation (PC): A PC is a structure specifically designed for professional service providers. It offers limited liability protection for the actions of individual members while maintaining a level of professional autonomy.

Consulting with a legal professional specializing in business structures for architectural firms will help you determine which structure suits your firm's goals and needs.

b. Intellectual Property Protection:
As architects, your designs and creations are your intellectual property. Protecting your work is essential to safeguard your professional reputation and potential financial interests. Here are key considerations:

   - Copyright: Copyright protection automatically applies to your original designs. However, registering your designs with the appropriate intellectual property office will provide additional legal protections.

   - Trademarks: Trademark registration can protect your firm's logo, name, or slogan, distinguishing it from competitors and preventing unauthorized use.

   - Patents: In some cases, your architectural innovations may be eligible for patent protection, granting exclusive rights for a defined period. Consult with a specialized intellectual property attorney to determine if patenting your design concepts is feasible and advisable.

Developing clear licensing agreements when sharing your designs or collaborating on projects is critical for protecting your intellectual assets and avoiding potential disputes.

c. Contracts and Agreements:

Contracts form the foundation of any architectural project, ensuring the rights, responsibilities, and expectations of all parties involved are clearly defined. Here are important contract considerations:

   - Owner-Architect Agreements: These contracts outline the scope of work, design fees, project timeline, and other crucial project-specific details. Understanding the risks, responsibilities, and contingencies is vital to protect your firm's interests.

   - Sub-Consultant Contracts: If you engage sub-consultants, it is important to have detailed contracts that clearly define their scope of services, deliverables, and payment terms.

   - Letter Agreements: This is a flexible option for smaller projects or specific design services.

It is important to clearly outline the terms, fees, and responsibilities of each party in a letter agreement.

- Indemnity and Insurance Requirements: Review insurance requirements imposed by clients, consultants, or third parties. Ensure your firm's liability and professional indemnity insurance align with contractual obligations.

- Dispute Resolution and Arbitration: Including dispute resolution mechanisms such as mediation or arbitration clauses in contracts can help manage potential conflicts and avoid costly litigation.
Leverage legal professionals experienced in architecture-related contracts to help you draft and negotiate agreements that protect your firm's interests while maintaining positive client relationships.

d. Professional Liability and Insurance:
Professional liability (PL) insurance is essential to protect your firm from claims arising from errors or omissions in your architectural services.

Consider the following:

- Coverage Considerations: Ensure your PL insurance covers not only your firm but also your employees, contractors, and sub-consultants. Tailor your coverage to adequately address potential risks related to your specific practice areas.

- Claim History: Review the PL insurance carrier's claim history and reputation before finalizing a policy. Choose an insurer with experience in the architectural industry to ensure they understand the unique risks you face.

- Contractual Requirements: Clients and project owners may require specific insurance coverage as part of the contract. Review these requirements carefully and ensure your insurance policy aligns with them.

- Risk Management: While insurance is crucial, implementing robust risk management practices can help prevent claims. Maintain clear communication with clients, document decisions and changes thoroughly, and regularly review your quality control processes.

- Professional Bodies and Associations: Joining professional bodies and associations, such as the American Institute of Architects (AIA), can provide access to resources, guidance, and network opportunities that support professional development and risk management.
Consult with insurance specialists knowledgeable in professional liability coverage to find the best-fit insurance policy for your firm's needs.

2. Financial Management:
a. Budgeting and Financial Planning:
A sound financial plan ensures your architectural firm's long-term stability and success. Consider the following aspects when developing your financial strategy:

   - Revenue Projections: Estimate your firm's recurring revenue streams, such as architectural fees, retainers, and royalties. Build in flexibility for fluctuations in project volume or duration.
   - Expense Budgeting: Identify your firm's fixed and variable costs, including office rent, utilities, employee salaries and benefits, software licenses, marketing expenses, professional

memberships, and continuing education. Regularly review and refine your budget to ensure accurate financial planning.

- Contingency Reserves: Setting aside funds for unforeseen expenses or contingencies is vital. Aim to maintain a reserve equal to a percentage of your annual expenses, providing a buffer during challenging times.

- Financial Goals: Establish short-term and long-term financial goals for your firm. These may include expanding your client base, increasing profitability, or investing in new technologies to enhance productivity.

- Financial Forecasting: Utilize financial forecasting techniques, such as cash flow projections and scenario analysis, to anticipate potential challenges or opportunities. This will enable proactive decision-making and help you steer your firm towards financial success.

- Cash Flow Management: Effectively monitoring and managing your cash flow is essential for financial stability. Implement strategies such as clear payment terms, efficient invoicing and follow-up processes, and optimization of accounts receivable and payable. Maintain a cash reserve and explore financing options when needed.

- Partnerships and Collaborations: Exploring strategic partnerships or collaborations with complementary firms or professionals can provide additional revenue streams and mutually beneficial growth opportunities.

- Tax Planning: Engage an experienced accountant or tax professional to help you optimize your tax planning strategies, explore deductions and incentives, and ensure compliance with tax regulations.

b. Project Cost Estimation and Fee Structures: Accurate project cost estimation and appropriate fee structures are essential for your firm's financial viability. Consider the following factors when determining your fees:

- Project Complexity and Scope: Evaluate each project's unique aspects, such as size, complexity, site conditions, and regulatory requirements. Projects with greater complexity may require higher fees to account for additional time, expertise, and resources.

- Time and Effort Estimates: Estimate the number of hours and resources required to complete a project. - Professional Fees: Calculate your fees based on the estimated project duration, hourly rates, and any additional factors such as travel expenses, design revisions, or specialized expertise.

- Fee Structures: Determine which fee structure best suits your firm's needs and the project's requirements. Common fee structures include:

- Percentage of Construction Cost: This fee structure charges a percentage of the total construction cost of the project. It is commonly used for larger projects.

- Hourly Billing: Billing clients based on the number of hours spent on the project, multiplied by the hourly rate.

- Fixed Fee: Charging a predetermined fixed fee for the entire project, regardless of the actual hours spent.

- Value-based Pricing: This approach considers the value of the architectural services provided and the potential benefits or cost savings for the client.

- Review Market Rates: Research market rates and the fees charged by other architectural firms in your region to ensure your fees are competitive yet profitable.

- Scope Creep: Clearly define the project scope in the contract to avoid scope creep and the need for additional unpaid work.

- Revisit Fee Structures: Regularly review and evaluate your fee structures to ensure they are aligned with the market, cover your costs, and provide a reasonable profit margin.

c. Cash Flow Management:
Effectively managing your firm's cash flow is essential for financial stability. Consider the following strategies:

- Invoicing: Establish clear and consistent invoicing processes, including invoicing promptly and accurately after project milestones or on a monthly basis.

- Payment Terms: Negotiate feasible and favorable payment terms with clients, such as requiring an upfront deposit or specifying payment dates and conditions in the contract.

- Accounts Receivable Management: Monitor your accounts receivable closely, following up on unpaid invoices promptly. Implement strategies to encourage timely payment, such as offering discounts for early payment or charging late fees for overdue invoices.

- Expense Control: Regularly review and analyze your firm's expenses to identify opportunities for cost-saving or optimization. Cut unnecessary expenses and negotiate better terms with suppliers whenever possible.

- Cash Reserve: Maintain a cash reserve to cover unexpected expenses or fluctuations in revenue. Consider setting aside a percentage of your revenue for this purpose.

- Financing Options: Explore financing options such as lines of credit, business loans, or leasing equipment to help manage cash flow during lean periods or when investing in growth opportunities.

- Forecasting and Projection: Utilize financial forecasting techniques to anticipate potential cash flow gaps or surpluses. This will enable you to make informed decisions, such as adjusting expenses or pursuing additional projects.

d. Tax Planning and Compliance:
Proper tax planning and compliance are crucial to avoid penalties and optimize your firm's financial position. Consider the following tax-related aspects:

- Engage a Tax Professional: Consult with a knowledgeable accountant or tax professional who specializes in the architectural industry. They can provide guidance on tax planning, deductions, and compliance requirements.
- Record Keeping: Maintain accurate and organized financial records, including receipts, invoices, bank statements, and expense reports. Proper record keeping will streamline tax preparation and facilitate compliance.
- Tax Deductions: Understand which business expenses are tax-deductible, such as office rent, employee salaries, professional development courses, marketing expenses, and travel costs. Maximize your deductions to minimize your tax liability.
- Tax Deadlines: Stay updated on tax filing and payment deadlines to avoid penalties. Set reminders or utilize digital accounting software

to help you stay organized.

- Entity-specific Taxes: Different legal structures may have different tax obligations. Consult with your tax professional to ensure compliance with entity-specific tax requirements.

- Tax Incentives and Credits: Research and take advantage of any tax incentives or credits available to architectural firms, such as energy-efficient design credits or research and development incentives.

- Quarterly Estimated Taxes: Architectural firms are typically required to make quarterly estimated tax payments to avoid underpayment penalties. Monitor your business income and consult with your tax professional to determine the required amounts.

Conclusion:

Navigating the legal and financial aspects of running an architectural firm requires careful planning, attention to detail, and a solid understanding of the industry's regulatory framework. Choosing the right legal structure, protecting your intellectual property, implementing strong contracts, acquiring professional liability insurance, and effectively managing your firm's finances are key considerations for long-term success. Seek guidance from legal and financial professionals with expertise in the architectural industry to ensure compliance and optimize your firm's financial stability and growth.

Strategies for Effective Marketing and Client Acquisition

In the competitive world of architecture, it is essential to have a strong marketing and client acquisition strategy in place to attract and retain clients. Your architectural firm may have the most talented architects and designers, but without effective marketing, your services may go unnoticed. In this chapter, we will delve into various strategies that can help you market your firm and acquire clients successfully.

1. Define Your Target Market:

Before you can effectively market your services, it is crucial to identify and understand your target market. Consider factors such as demographics, geographic location, industry specialization, and psychographic characteristics. By understanding your target market's needs, preferences, and pain points, you can tailor your marketing efforts to reach the right audience. For instance, if your firm specializes in sustainable design, your target

market may include environmentally conscious clients, such as eco-friendly organizations or homeowners looking to build sustainable residences. By narrowing your focus to specific niches within the architecture industry, you can position your firm as an expert in that particular area, attracting clients who seek specialized expertise.

2. Develop a Strong Brand Identity:

Your firm's brand identity is more than just a logo or a tagline - it is the overall perception that clients have of your business. To develop a strong brand identity, start by defining your firm's vision, mission, and core values. Consider how you want to be perceived and what unique value proposition you bring to the market. With this foundation, invest time in creating a compelling brand story, visual identity, and messaging that resonates with your target audience. Ensure consistency across all marketing channels to establish a strong and recognizable brand. Consider how you can differentiate your firm from competitors.

What unique values, design philosophy, or approach do you bring to the table?

Communicating this differentiation clearly will attract clients who align with your firm's vision and values.

3. Build an Engaging Online Presence:

In today's digital age, having a strong online presence is essential for any business. Create a modern and user-friendly website that showcases your projects, highlights your expertise, and provides easy ways for potential clients to contact you. Your website should have a clear and intuitive navigation structure, visually appealing images of your work, and engaging content. Utilize search engine optimization (SEO) techniques to improve your website's visibility in search engine results. Research and incorporate relevant keywords in your website content to increase organic traffic. Additionally, leverage social media platforms to share your work, connect with potential clients, and engage in relevant industry conversations. Develop a

content calendar to consistently share valuable content, such as project updates, industry insights, or design tips, through blog posts, videos, or infographics.

Engage with your audience by responding to comments, initiating conversations, and showcasing your expertise. Actively participate in online architecture communities and forums to establish yourself as a knowledgeable professional and build trust within your target market.

4. Leverage Content Marketing:

Showcasing your firm's expertise through valuable content can position you as a thought leader in the industry. Research industry trends, challenges, and emerging topics to develop content that addresses your target market's needs and interests. Write blog posts, whitepapers, or case studies that provide insights into your design process, sustainability practices, architectural trends, or any other relevant topics. By sharing your knowledge and

expertise, you not only demonstrate your capabilities but also build trust with potential clients. Focus on providing value rather than just promoting your services. Additionally, consider guest posting on industry websites or participating in podcast interviews to further expand your reach and establish your credibility. Collaborate with influencers or industry experts to co-create content that can reach a wider audience. By consistently providing valuable and educational content, you will attract clients who appreciate your expertise and approach.

5. Network and Collaborate:

Building strong relationships with other professionals in the industry can lead to valuable referrals and collaborations. Attend industry conferences, join professional organizations, and participate in networking events to connect with potential clients and partners. Actively seek opportunities to engage with influential individuals and decision-makers in your target market. Create meaningful connections by actively engaging in

conversations, offering insights, and providing value to others. Collaboration with other professionals, such as interior designers, engineers, or construction firms, can expand your service offerings and attract clients who prefer integrated solutions. Consider forming partnerships or participating in joint marketing initiatives with complementary businesses to leverage each other's networks and increase brand exposure.

6. Utilize Traditional Marketing Methods:

While digital marketing is vital, traditional marketing methods should not be overlooked. Explore opportunities to showcase your work through print media, such as architectural magazines or local newspapers. Advertise in industry-specific directories or sponsor relevant events to increase visibility within your target market. Collaborate with local organizations or nonprofits to support community initiatives and gain exposure. Additionally, consider hosting or participating in design workshops or seminars to demonstrate your expertise and attract potential clients who prefer more interactive experiences. Engaging in traditional marketing channels can help you reach a wider audience and create brand recognition in both online and offline environments.

7. Develop a Referral Program:

Encourage satisfied clients to refer your services to their acquaintances by implementing a referral program. Word-of-mouth marketing is incredibly powerful, as recommendations from trusted sources carry significant weight. Offer incentives, such as discounts on future projects or exclusive access to events, to clients who refer new business to your firm. Implement a systematic approach to track and reward referrals, ensuring that clients feel appreciated for their contributions. Additionally, consider reaching out to past clients for testimonials or case studies that can be featured on your website to build trust and credibility. Authentic testimonials, backed by real client experiences, are invaluable in establishing your reputation and attracting new clients.

8. Track and Analyze Results:

To continuously improve your marketing efforts, track and analyze the results of your campaigns. Utilize web analytics tools to measure website traffic, user behavior, and conversions. Monitor the success of your social media posts, email campaigns, or other marketing initiatives, and adjust your strategies accordingly. Collect feedback from clients and prospects to gain insights into their motivations, pain points, and preferences. Data-driven insights will help you understand which channels and tactics are most effective in reaching and engaging your target audience. Regularly review and update your marketing plan based on the data to maximize your return on investment.

Conclusion:

Marketing an architectural firm requires a multifaceted approach that combines online and offline strategies. By defining your target market, developing a strong brand identity, building an engaging online presence,

leveraging content marketing, networking and collaborating, utilizing traditional marketing methods, developing a referral program, and tracking and analyzing results, you can effectively market your firm and acquire new clients.

Remember, marketing is an ongoing process that requires consistent effort and adaptability. By implementing these strategies and staying attuned to the evolving needs of your target market, you can ensure the success and growth of your architectural firm.

The Art of Project Management: From Concept to Completion

Project management is an essential skill for architects. It involves overseeing and coordinating all aspects of a project, from its initial concept to its final completion. Effective project management ensures that a project is delivered on time, within budget, and meets the client's expectations. In this chapter, we will explore the art of project management in the context of architecture and discuss key strategies and best practices.

1. Planning and Scope Definition:
   - Before embarking on any project, it is crucial to define the project's scope and objectives. This involves understanding the client's requirements, constraints, and desired outcomes.
   - Conduct a comprehensive needs assessment in collaboration with the client to understand their vision, goals, and purpose for the project.
   - Develop a detailed project plan, including timelines, resource allocation, and deliverables. This plan will serve as a roadmap for the project's execution and provide a reference point for progress tracking.
   - Identify key project stakeholders and establish clear lines of communication and engagement.

2. Team Building and Collaboration:
   - As an architect, you will work with a diverse team of professionals, including engineers, contractors, and suppliers. Building and managing an effective team is vital for project success.
   - Select team members based on their expertise, experience, and compatibility with the project requirements.
   - Foster open communication and collaboration among team members. Encourage the sharing of ideas and solutions, and establish clear roles and responsibilities to ensure smooth workflow and accountability.
   - Conduct regular team meetings to align on project objectives, resolve any conflicts or challenges, and reinforce a sense of shared purpose.

3. Risk Management:
   - Identify potential risks and develop mitigation strategies. This includes anticipating challenges, such as budgetary constraints, design changes, or unforeseen circumstances, and having contingency plans in place.
   - Conduct a thorough risk analysis to identify potential pitfalls and devise strategies to minimize their impact on the project.
   - Regularly assess and monitor project risks throughout its lifecycle. Be prepared to adapt and adjust strategies as needed to ensure project success.
   - Engage in proactive communication with

stakeholders to manage their expectations and address potential risks and uncertainties.

4. Budget and Cost Control:
   - Monitor project costs and ensure adherence to the allocated budget. Establish a system for tracking expenses and controlling costs, including regular financial reporting and analysis.
   - Develop a comprehensive cost estimate by considering factors such as material prices, labor costs, permits, and potential hidden expenses.
   - Proactively identify potential cost-saving opportunities without compromising the project's quality, such as exploring alternative materials or construction methods.
   - Implement effective change management processes to evaluate and approve any scope or budget changes, ensuring transparency and accountability.

5. Time Management:
   - Develop a detailed project schedule with clearly defined milestones and deadlines. Regularly track progress against the schedule and make adjustments as necessary.
   - Efficiently manage time by prioritizing tasks, delegating responsibilities, and establishing realistic timelines for each phase of the project.
   - Use project management software or tools to automate scheduling, task allocation, and progress tracking, improving efficiency and coordination

among team members.
  - Foster a culture of accountability and time-consciousness among the project team, emphasizing the importance of meeting deadlines and milestones.

6. Client Communication and Expectation Management:
  - Maintain open and transparent communication with the client throughout the project. Regularly provide updates on progress, address any concerns or issues, and manage expectations.
  - Actively involve the client in the decision-making process, ensuring their input is considered and incorporated when appropriate.
  - Establish clear channels of communication, such as regular meetings or digital collaboration platforms, to facilitate effective and timely communication with the client.
  - Provide the client with a platform to review and validate key project deliverables, ensuring alignment and minimizing the potential for misunderstandings or revisions.

7. Quality Assurance:
  - Ensure that the project meets high standards of quality and craftsmanship. Regularly review and inspect the work to ensure compliance with design specifications and industry standards.
  - Implement quality control measures throughout the construction process by conducting site visits and coordinating with contractors, subcontractors,

and suppliers.

- Use quality management tools and techniques to identify and address any potential quality issues, ensuring the project's successful completion to the client's satisfaction.

- Establish quality benchmarks and performance indicators to measure and assess the project's

progress and quality at various stages.

8. Documentation and Record-Keeping:

- Maintain accurate and organized project documentation, including drawings, contracts, permits, and correspondence. This will facilitate effective communication, as well as serve as a reference for future projects.

- Document all changes and revisions to the project's scope, budget, or timeline. Keep a log of decisions made, design modifications, and any other project-related information to ensure accountability and avoid misunderstandings.

- Utilize project management software or cloud-based platforms to store and manage project documentation securely, allowing easy access and collaboration among team members.

- Establish clear protocols for document control and version management to avoid confusion or discrepancies in project-related documentation.

9. Stakeholder Management:

- Consider the project's impact on various stakeholders, including the client, end-users, community, and regulatory authorities. Engage in effective stakeholder management to ensure their needs and concerns are addressed.

   - Maintain regular communication with stakeholders, providing updates on project progress, addressing any issues or changes, and seeking their input when necessary.

   - Anticipate and manage potential conflicts or conflicts of interest among stakeholders, ensuring a

collaborative and harmonious project environment.

   - Proactively engage with local community members and relevant authorities to understand and comply with applicable regulations, codes, and standards.

10. Lessons Learned and Continuous Improvement:

   - Reflect on each project's outcomes and feedback received from all stakeholders to identify lessons learned and areas for improvement.

   - Conduct project post-mortems or debriefing sessions to facilitate team discussions and identify best practices, challenges, and opportunities for growth.

   - Document key takeaways and incorporate them into future project planning and execution to enhance the overall project management process.

   - Continuously seek professional development opportunities to stay abreast of new project management trends, technologies, and methodologies.

In summary, effective project management is critical in architecture to ensure successful project delivery. By carefully planning, building a strong team, managing risks and costs, maintaining open communication with clients, assuring quality, documenting processes, managing stakeholders effectively, and incorporating continuous improvement practices, architects can navigate the complexities of project management and bring their creative visions to life.

Fostering Innovation and Creativity in Architectural Practice

In today's highly connected world, networking and collaboration have become essential tools for success in the architectural industry. The power of strategic partnerships cannot be underestimated, as it can open doors to new opportunities, expand your professional network, and enhance the credibility of your architectural firm. In this chapter, we will delve deeper into the various ways you can harness the potential of networking and collaboration to propel your firm's growth to new heights.

1. Building Authentic Relationships:
Networking goes beyond mere transactions and

business cards; it is about building genuine connections with like-minded individuals and firms in the industry. To establish authentic relationships, it requires a proactive approach. Attending industry events, conferences, and workshops provides a unique opportunity to meet fellow architects, developers, contractors, and other professionals. Engaging in meaningful

conversations, actively listening, and showing genuine interest in others' work are key to forging strong connections. Networking events not only offer the chance to meet potential clients but also enable you to establish relationships with peers who can refer clients to your firm in the future. After the event, make sure to follow up with your new contacts, nurturing the relationship through regular communication and sharing valuable industry insights.

Nurturing existing relationships is equally important. Maintaining regular contact with your

professional network through emails, social media interactions, or occasional meetings for coffee or lunch goes a long way. By staying connected and showing a genuine interest in their endeavors, you can foster relationships that can lead to valuable collaborations and referrals in the future.

2. Collaborating on Projects:

Strategic partnerships often involve collaborating on projects with firms that complement your expertise and share a similar

work philosophy. Collaborations can be undertaken for specific projects or as ongoing partnerships. It is beneficial to seek out firms that specialize in different aspects of architecture, such as interior design, landscape architecture, or sustainable design. By combining your skills and knowledge, you can offer clients a comprehensive and integrated approach to their architectural needs.

When considering a collaboration, establishing clear objectives, responsibilities, and

expectations from the outset is crucial. Determine the roles and contributions of each partner and define how decisions will be made and project responsibilities shared. Effective communication and a shared vision are essential for a successful collaboration. Regular progress updates and meetings should be scheduled to keep all parties informed and engaged throughout the project.

Collaborative projects not only enhance the quality of your work but also provide opportunities for cross-promotion and exposure to new markets.

Celebrating successful collaborations by

sharing the project's achievements on social media and professional networks expands the reach of both firms involved, attracting new clients and fostering a positive reputation for future collaborations.

3. Joint Marketing Initiatives:
Partnering with other firms for marketing initiatives can be a powerful tool in expanding

your reach and attracting new clients. These joint initiatives can include co-hosting events, sharing content on each other's platforms, or even launching joint advertising campaigns. By leveraging the client base and resources of your partners, you can achieve greater visibility and generate more leads for your firm.

To ensure effective joint marketing initiatives, aligning marketing goals and strategies with your partners Is essential. Identify the target audience and craft a cohesive message that resonates with both firms' brand identities. This can be achieved through collaborative brainstorming sessions where creative ideas flow, resulting in unique marketing strategies.

Highlighting each partner's strengths and expertise creates a win-win situation for both firms involved.

4. Participating in Industry Associations:
Joining industry associations and professional

organizations can be an excellent way to network and collaborate with other architects in

your region or specialization. These associations often organize networking events, conferences, seminars, and trade shows where you can meet potential partners and stay updated on industry trends. Active participation in such associations can enhance your professional reputation and open doors to speaking engagements or leadership positions, further expanding your network and influence.

Industry associations provide a platform to exchange ideas and best practices with peers, fostering a culture of collaboration rather than competition. Engage in panel discussions or present case studies at industry conferences to showcase your expertise and establish yourself as a thought leader in the field. By actively contributing to the industry, you can attract like-minded professionals who are eager to collaborate and collectively elevate the architectural profession.

5. Mentoring and Knowledge Sharing: Networking is not only about what you can gain but also about what you can offer.

As an established architect, consider mentoring young professionals or offering internships to aspiring architects. Sharing your knowledge and experiences not only helps the next generation of architects but also creates opportunities for collaboration and partnership in the future. Actively contribute to forums, blog posts, or publication articles by providing valuable insights and expertise to the architectural community.

Become a respected mentor and thought leader in the industry by offering guidance, support, and feedback to emerging professionals. Mentoring relationships can extend beyond the initial mentorship phase, leading to long-lasting collaborations or referrals. By fostering a culture of knowledge sharing and collaboration within the industry, you can attract talented individuals and firms who value your expertise and are eager to collaborate.

In conclusion, networking and collaboration are essential strategies for architects looking to grow their practice and thrive in a competitive industry. By building authentic relationships, collaborating on projects, engaging in joint marketing initiatives, participating in industry associations, and embracing mentorship and knowledge sharing, you can harness the power of strategic partnerships to propel your firm's success. Embrace the opportunities that networking presents, and be open to collaborative ventures that can expand your horizons and elevate your architectural practice to new heights. Let your partnerships flourish, and together, let's shape the future of architecture.

Collaborating with Other Professionals and Industry Partners

Collaboration is the backbone of success in the field of architecture. As an architect, your ability to work seamlessly with other professionals and industry partners is essential for bringing your designs to life. Effective collaboration can lead to innovative and exceptional results, while poor collaboration can result in delays, misunderstandings, and ultimately a compromised project. In this chapter, we will delve deeper into the crucial aspects of successful collaboration and provide strategies for fostering productive partnerships.

1. Building Strong Relationships:

Developing strong relationships with other professionals and industry partners is fundamental to successful collaboration. Building these relationships involves more than just networking. It starts with clear and open communication along with a foundation of mutual respect. Take the time to understand each other's roles, responsibilities, and expertise. By establishing trust and understanding, you can create an environment conducive to collaboration. A network of trusted professionals whose skills complement your own will greatly enhance the collaborative process.

2. Recognizing the Value of Expertise:

Collaboration allows architects to tap into the specialized expertise of various professionals, enriching the overall design process. Engage and involve professionals such as structural engineers, interior designers, landscape architects, and contractors at the appropriate stages of the project. By appreciating and integrating their expertise, architects can create more comprehensive and holistic designs that surpass expectations.

Structural engineers bring their knowledge in analyzing the structural integrity of the design, ensuring that it meets safety standards. Interior designers contribute their expertise in space planning, aesthetics, and functionality, helping to create spaces that are visually appealing and functional. Landscape architects enhance the external environment of the project, considering factors such as site features, vegetation, and sustainability. Collaborating with contractors early on helps ensure that the design is practical to construct and within budget. By embracing the value of expertise, architects can elevate their designs to a new level.

3. Establishing Common Goals and Objectives:

Before commencing any collaboration, it is essential to establish clear and shared goals and objectives. A clearly defined project vision and scope ensure that all parties involved are aligned from the outset. Establishing common goals allows for a unified approach, fostering teamwork and minimizing conflicts. Regular meetings and open communication channels enable ongoing collaboration and reaffirm the collective understanding of the project's direction. Documenting these goals and objectives in a comprehensive project brief serves as a reference point throughout the project and allows for accountability and focus.

4. Clear Communication:

Communication lies at the heart of effective collaboration. Architects must establish a robust communication framework that facilitates frequent and open dialogue. This can be achieved through regular meetings, video conferences, emails, or project management software. Clear communication ensures that everyone involved is aware of project progress, potential challenges, and required decisions. Regularly sharing relevant project information and updates is crucial in maintaining transparency and avoiding misunderstandings.

In addition to regular communication channels, architects should also establish structured systems for documenting and sharing project information. Utilizing cloud-based platforms and project management tools can help streamline communication and ensure that all stakeholders have access to the most up-to-date information. Clear and accessible communication allows for efficient collaboration, ensuring that all parties are working towards the same objectives.

5. Embracing a Team Approach:

Successful collaboration fosters a sense of unity and teamwork among all project participants. It is essential to create an environment where all team members feel valued and engaged in the decision-making process. Emphasize a culture of respect, trust, and collaboration, allowing diverse perspectives and ideas to flourish. Engage in active listening, promoting constructive feedback, and celebrating collective achievements. By embracing a team approach, architects foster collaboration and empower team members to contribute their expertise and unique perspectives. This inclusive and collaborative environment leads to the most creative and innovative design solutions.

6. Managing Conflicts:

Conflicts are inevitable in any collaborative effort, but they can be managed effectively through proactive conflict resolution strategies. It is essential to identify and address conflicts early on to prevent escalation and minimize negative impacts on the project. Encourage open and respectful discussions to understand the root causes of conflicts and work towards mutually beneficial solutions. Engaging in active problem-solving, mediation, or involving a neutral third party can facilitate constructive conflict resolution, ensuring that the collaborative process remains productive.

When conflicts arise, it is crucial to approach them with a mindset of finding a resolution that benefits the project and all stakeholders involved. By fostering a culture of open communication and respect, conflicts can be seen as an opportunity for growth and improvement rather than a hindrance to collaboration.

7. Continuous Learning and Improvement:

Collaboration offers architects an opportunity for continuous learning and improvement. Reflect on each collaborative project, evaluating what worked well and areas that require enhancement. Foster a culture of continuous improvement by sharing lessons learned within the team. This can be achieved through post-project reviews, personal and professional development opportunities, and establishing a knowledge-sharing culture. Embrace new technologies, design methodologies, and industry trends to stay at the forefront of architectural innovation.

Architects should actively seek feedback from colleagues and project partners to understand areas where their collaborative skills can be further honed. Actively participate in industry events, conferences, and workshops to stay updated on emerging trends and best practices in collaboration. By embracing a growth mindset and continually learning and improving, architects can enhance their collaborative skills and drive the success of their projects.

In conclusion, successful collaboration with other professionals and industry partners is paramount for architects to excel in their practice. Building strong relationships, recognizing the value of expertise, establishing clear goals, and maintaining open communication form the foundation of effective collaboration. Embrace a team approach, navigate conflicts gracefully, and continuously learn and improve from each collaborative project. By doing so, architects can elevate the quality of their architectural designs and make a lasting impact on the built environment.

Scaling Up Your Architectural Firm: Growth Strategies and Expansion Opportunities

The architectural industry is continuously evolving, and as a writer in this field, it is crucial to stay ahead of the curve by embracing new and innovative marketing approaches. In this chapter, we will explore some future trends expected to shape the landscape of architectural marketing and provide in-depth insights into how architects can adapt and leverage these trends to their advantage.

1. Immersive Technologies:

Immersive technologies such as virtual reality (VR) and augmented reality (AR) have revolutionized the architectural industry. Architects can now create virtual walkthroughs, allowing clients to experience their designs in a realistic and engaging manner. This not only enhances the visual representation of projects but also enables architects to showcase their creativity and gives clients a better

understanding of the end result.

By immersing clients in a virtual environment, architects can effectively communicate the spatial qualities, materiality, and overall aesthetics of their designs. Embracing VR and AR in marketing efforts can greatly improve communication, decision-making, and client satisfaction.

2. Sustainability and Green Building Practices:

There is a growing awareness of climate change and the need for sustainable design solutions in the architectural industry. Architects who prioritize sustainable and environmentally friendly practices are more likely to attract environmentally conscious clients. By highlighting their commitment to sustainability in their marketing efforts, architects can position themselves as leaders who contribute to a more sustainable future. Certification programs such as LEED (Leadership in Energy and Environmental Design) and WELL Building Standard can further strengthen their credibility and appeal to a broader client base interested

in sustainable and eco-friendly design.

Architects can showcase their expertise in energy-efficient strategies, renewable materials, water conservation, and green building practices while educating clients about the long-term benefits of sustainable design.

3. Personalization:

Advancements in data collection and analytics

enable architects to gather valuable information about their clients' preferences, needs, and lifestyles. By utilizing this data effectively, architects can tailor their marketing messages and design solutions to meet the specific requirements of each client. Personalization goes beyond surface-level customization; it involves understanding the unique aspirations, values, and lifestyles of clients to create spaces that truly resonate with their personalities. Architects can employ strategies such as user surveys, interviews, and interactive workshops to gather insights and co-create designs with their clients. Through personalization, architects can offer unique design experiences, cater to

individual tastes, and nurture long-term partnerships based on mutual trust and understanding.

4. Social Media Presence:

In today's digital age, social media has become an essential tool for architects to showcase their work and connect with potential clients. Platforms like Instagram, Pinterest, and Houzz allow architects to share high-quality visuals, behind-the-scenes content, and engaging storytelling to reach a wider audience. Building an online brand presence, engaging with potential clients, and fostering a sense of community can help architects establish themselves as authorities in the field and attract new business opportunities. It is important for architects to curate a visually compelling and cohesive social media presence that reflects their unique style, expertise, and values. By interacting with followers, responding to inquiries, and participating in relevant industry conversations, architects can build a loyal online following and increase their chances of being

discovered by potential clients.

5. Marketing Automation and Artificial Intelligence (AI):

Staying up to date with emerging trends in marketing automation and AI can give architects a competitive advantage. Automation tools streamline and optimize various marketing processes, allowing architects to focus more on their core expertise. From email campaigns and lead nurturing to analytics and lead management, automation platforms can handle routine tasks efficiently, freeing up more time for architects to focus on design and client relationships. AI-powered chatbots and virtual assistants can enhance the customer experience by providing instant assistance, personalized recommendations, and efficient communication. Integrating automation and AI into marketing strategies can help architects improve efficiency, responsiveness, and overall client satisfaction, while also staying organized and maximizing their marketing efforts.

6. Collaborative and Transparent Approach:

Clients today seek a more collaborative and transparent approach from architects.

By involving clients in the design process, architects can build trust and ensure that the final outcome aligns with their vision. Emphasizing collaboration and transparency in marketing efforts can attract clients who value open communication, co-creation, and a sense of ownership in the design process. Architects can adopt communication tools and collaborative platforms to facilitate seamless interactions and transparent sharing of design concepts, progress updates, and budgetary considerations. This approach not only enhances client satisfaction but also leads to positive word-of-mouth referrals and long-term partnerships. Clients who feel heard, included, and respected during the design process are more likely to become advocates for the architect's work.

In conclusion, the future of architectural marketing lies in embracing innovative approaches that leverage technology,

sustainability, personalization, social media, automation, and collaboration. As a writer in the industry, it is essential to recognize these future trends and provide architects with the knowledge and guidance to adapt and thrive in this dynamic landscape. By embracing new technologies, prioritizing sustainability, personalizing their approach, leveraging social media, embracing automation and AI, and adopting a collaborative and transparent mindset, architects can navigate the ever-changing landscape of architectural marketing successfully, secure a prominent position in the industry, and leave a lasting impact through their projects.

www.ingramcontent.com/pod-product-compliance
Lightning Source LLC
Chambersburg PA
CBHW062353290526
45794CB00005B/2210